Learning with Dotard

(The Art of the Presidency)

TWEET TWEET TWEET

By Susan Thaemlitz and Craig Stuart
Illustrated by Dack Stevens

D1209360

No women or minorities were assaulted, insulted or deported in the making of this book.

Learning with Dotard (The Art of the Presidency)
Copyright © 2017 by Little Big League, LLC

All rights reserved. No part of this book may be reproduced or transmitted in any form or by any means, electronic or mechanical, including photocopying, recording, or by any information storage and retrieval system, without permission in writing from the publisher.

Published by Little Big League, LLC

ISBN: 978-0-692-98970-8

Dedicated to our nephews,
Vincent and Charlie. May you grow up
in a world less divisive, filled
with love and compassion.

Special thanks goes out to our amazing illustrator, Dack Stevens.
A book without illustrations is like biscuits without gravy.
Your illustrations have lifted this project to another level.
Everything we cannot say with words you have expressed with your imagination and humor.
Thanks for the support and contributions from our friends Jen V., Eric K., Mark F., Matt M.
and our printing friends at Graphx Connection, Inc.

Do•tard \ **DOH**-terd \ noun:

a person, especially an old person, exhibiting a decline in mental faculties;
a weak-minded or foolish old person.

Sentence example:
"I will surely and definitely tame the mentally deranged U.S. dotard with fire."

"We're going to win so much,
you're going to be so sick and
tired of winning."

Winning

 Truth Bomb:

His companies have filed for Chapter 11 bankruptcy protection on six different occasions.

Macy's dumped his clothing line in 2015.

On August 13, 2017, The Celebrity Apprentice was officially cancelled.

He lost the popular vote in the presidential 2016 election by a bigger margin than any other president in U.S. history. He received 62,979,879 votes and his opponent received 65,844,954 votes.

"This is an ISLAND, surrounded by water. Big water. Ocean water."

Geography of Puerto Rico

Island

Water

Big Water

Ocean Water

 Truth Bomb:

All islands are surrounded by water – that's what makes them islands.

"I will tell you I left Texas and I left Florida and I left Louisiana and I went to Puerto Rico and I met with the president of the Virgin Islands."

 Truth Bomb:

Um ... He IS the president of the Virgin Islands.

"I give ourselves a ten."
– on response to the Puerto Rico Hurricane

 Truth Bomb:

Hurricane Maria hit Puerto Rico on September 20, 2017.
Two months later, more than half of the island was still without power.
This is the largest and longest blackout in U.S. history.

"Why can't we use nuclear weapons?"

Truth Bomb:

The effects of radiation on human beings cause suffering and death many years after the initial explosion.

The following are a few of the medical issues that would be epidemic:

- Eye Cataracts
- Blood disorders
- Infertility
- Infectious diseases
- Leukemia and many other types of cancers

"I would build a great wall
– and nobody builds walls better than me, believe me –
and I'll build them very inexpensively.
I will build a great, great wall on our southern border,
and I will have Mexico pay for that wall.
Mark my words."

Truth Bomb:

40% of undocumented immigrants travel by plane and overstay their visas.

Mexico never made a deal to pay for the wall and has openly refused to pay for any wall between the U.S. and Mexico.

The number of unauthorized immigrants living in the U.S. was lower in 2015 than in 2007, with the number of Mexican immigrants declining, and the number from other countries rising.

"The beauty of me is that I'm very rich."

 Truth Bomb:

That's what she said!

"Sorry losers and haters,
but my I.Q. is one of the highest – and you
all know it! Please don't feel stupid
or insecure, it's not your fault."

Truth Bomb:

His true intelligence quotient is unknown.

Common traits of highly intelligent people:

- They're highly adaptable and open-minded
- They understand how much they don't know
- They have unquenchable curiosity
- They have a high degree of self-control
- They're sensitive to other people's experiences

You be the judge.

"My fingers are long and beautiful,
as, it has been well documented,
are various other parts of my body."

 Truth Bomb:
Research has shown there is no correlation between finger length and the size of other body parts.

"We had a massive crowd of people. We had a crowd. I looked over that sea of people and I said to myself, 'WOW.' And I've seen crowds before. Big, big crowds. That was some crowd. When I looked at the numbers that happened to come in from all of the various sources, we had the biggest audience in the history of inaugural speeches."

Obama Crowd

Dotard Crowd

 Truth Bomb:

Estimated attendance for past inaugurations:

- Trump, 2017   250,000-600,000
- Obama, 2013   1,000,000
- Obama, 2009   1,800,000
- Bush, 2005   400,000
- Bush, 2001   300,000
- Cinton, 1997   250,000
- Cinton, 1993   800,000

"Eventually we're going to get something done and it's going to be really, really good."

 Truth Bomb:

Campaign Promise List:

☐ Repeal and replace Obamacare
☑ Defund Planned Parenthood
☐ Drain the swamp
☐ Balance federal budget
☐ Border wall (Mexico pays the bill)
☐ Release tax returns
☑ Refute climate change
☐ Make America great again

"I just want to stay in the White House
and work my ass off...."

 # Truth Bomb:

It has been confirmed he played 34 rounds of golf
in the first 11 months of his presidency.
Each trip costs taxpayers an estimated one million
to three million dollars.

"This is more work than in my previous life.
I thought it would be easier."

 Truth Bomb:
Being president of the United States IS harder than being a real estate mogul, executive TV producer, reality TV personality or celebrity groper.

"(Vladimir Putin) is not going into Ukraine, OK, just so you understand. He's not gonna go into Ukraine, all right? You can mark it down. You can put it down." - July 2016

Ukraine in 2014

 Truth Bomb:
Russian President Vladimir Putin seized control
of the Crimean Peninsula from Ukraine in early 2014.

"I think apologizing's a great thing, but
you have to be wrong. I will absolutely apologize,
sometime in the hopefully distant future,
if I am ever wrong."

An 'extremely credible source' has called my office and told me that @BarackObama's birth certificate is a fraud.

← 6,789 ⇄ 24,785 ★ 19,425

The concept of global warming was created by and for the Chinese in order to make U.S. manufacturing non-competitive.

← 13,723 ⇄ 101,598 ★ 69,735

Our Southern border is unsecure. I am the only one that can fix it, nobody else has the guts to even talk about it.

← 28,359 ⇄ 56,325 ★ 100,438

Nobody could have done what I've done for #PuertoRico with so little appreciation. So much work!

← 19,976 ⇄ 64,785 ★ 125,455

In addition to winning the Electoral College in a landslide, I won the popular vote if you deduct the millions of people who voted illegally

← 106,559 ⇄ 98,469 ★ 99,445

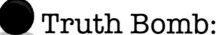 Truth Bomb:

We are still waiting for an apology …

"I'm a person that wants to tell the truth.
I'm an honest person, and what I'm saying,
you know is exactly right."

 Truth Bomb:

As of December 1, 2017, Fact Checker has catalogued 1,628 false or misleading claims by him since he took office in January 2017.

"Because I was down there and I watched our police and our firemen down at 7/11, down at the World Trade Center right after it came down. And I saw the greatest people I've ever seen in action."

Truth Bomb:

7-Eleven is an American-Japanese international chain of convenience stores, headquartered in Irving, Texas, and best known for its slurpees.

New York's finest responded to the terrorist attack on 9/11. A date the rest of us will never forget.

"Happy Cinco de Mayo!
The best taco bowls are made
in Trump Tower Grill.
I love Hispanics."

Bomba de Verdad:

According to Yelp, Trump Tower is not even ranked in the top 50 for taco bowls in New York City. Instead, we recommend you check out Nacho Macho Taco on 5th Avenue.

"It is time to drain the swamp in Washington, D.C. This is why I'm proposing a package of ethics reforms to make our government honest once again."

Truth Bomb:

The swamp is overflowing with corporate conflicts of interest, including 49 lobbyists who now work for agencies they used to lobby.

Twenty former lobbyists now work for the executive office of the president.

Despite criticizing other politicians for their relationships with Goldman Sachs, the president hired five former Goldman Sachs executives.

"What a nice sound that is.
Are they playing that for you or for me?"

Truth Bomb:

It is not everyday that the commander in chief is confused upon hearing a bugle playing "Retreat." It is not played for the president; rather, it is played every evening at 5 p.m. on every American Army installation to signal the end of the duty day and pay respect to the flag.

"I've had a beautiful,
I've had a flawless campaign.
You'll be writing books
about this campaign."

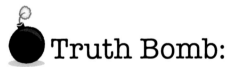 Truth Bomb:

Everybody loves *Learning with Dotard*!

Quotes from Past Presidents

"A house divided against itself cannot stand."
- Abraham Lincoln

"It is amazing what you can accomplish
when you do not care who gets the credit."
- Harry Truman

"Always give your best, never get discouraged, never be
petty; always remember, others may hate you, but those
who hate you don't win unless you hate them, and then
you destroy yourself."
- Richard Nixon